God Focused Devotions

Being Dazzled by God in Your Daily Bible Reading

God-Focused Devotions: Being Dazzled by God in Your Daily Bible Reading

By Frank Hamrick

Copyright © 2009 by Positive Action For Christ, Inc. P.O. Box 700, 502 W. Pippen Street, Whitakers, NC 27891-0700. All rights reserved. No part may be reproduced in any manner without permission in writing from the publisher.

Printed in the United States of America

ISBN: 978-1-59557-104-5

Edited by C.J. Harris

Layout and Design by Shannon Brown

Published by

Table of Content

Preface

"I know I need to have devotions," the teenager told me, "but, Frank, they just don't work for me! I don't get anything out of them."

I've heard this story often in my ministry with teens. But, I'll let you in on a secret—*they haven't always worked for me either!* Let's be honest, devotions can be downright boring! I know. I've tried just about every type of devotions known to man over the last 30 years. I found that, for the most part, my devotions just left me cold. I sometimes got something out of them, but more often than not, I was just "going through the motions."

Something was missing. I wasn't being dazzled by my devotions. Yet, Psalm 1 speaks of being "blessed" by meditating in the law of God day and night. Furthermore, Joshua was promised that he would have "good success" if he meditated in the law of the Lord day and night (Joshua 1:8). Somehow I didn't get that same "blessing" and "success" when I tried. Rather than being dazzled by my devotions, I was depressed, deflated, and defeated by them! Until…. I learned a secret right before my eyes!

All the time I had been having devotions, I had missed one major point. I was studying the Bible, learning facts, looking for a verse to help me live another day, when, instead, I was supposed to be enjoying God! I found that my devotions had been all about me—what *I* needed to learn, or what *I* needed to do, or where *I* had failed. My devotions were "me" centered.

But that wasn't how David had devotions, nor was it how Asaph, David's chief musician, had devotions. Their devotions were "God" focused. Psalm 27:4 was but one example. There David stated that he sought after one thing—that he might "behold" (literally, meditate on) the beauty of the Lord. In Psalm 63 David declared that he would remember God upon his bed and meditate on God in the night. That, to me, was interesting. David looked at the Bible as a tool to reveal the glory of his God—and he read it that way, looking for God in every passage he read.

This focus changed my devotions forever. My devotions came alive and led to joy and praise as I learned how to look for the glory and majesty of God in His Word. I got my eyes off of self and onto Him. Paradoxically, the more I saw Him, the more I saw my own sinful self. As Isaiah of old, who saw the Lord "high and lifted up," cried in response, "Woe is me," so my life began to change as I became entranced with a biblical view of God's person and works.

What about you? Perhaps you're a new Christian, and this is your first attempt to learn how to have effective devotions. Or perhaps you, like me, have tried different devotional methods and found most of them leaving you flat, or bored. Maybe this is yet one more attempt to get something meaningful from your devotions. Whatever the case, this booklet is for you!

The first three chapters are very important. They show you what having devotions is all about, and they show you why devotions often don't dazzle. But more importantly, they show you how to have exciting, thrilling devotions that make you hungry for more!

After these initial chapters, which teach you how to have great devotions, we have included twelve full weeks of devotions. During those twelve weeks you will begin with basic devotions and gradually move to more advanced devotions. In the beginning, you will simply learn how to read and discover truths about God in the Word. The later weeks will concentrate more and more on God's glorious character and works. By the end of the twelve weeks, you will have learned how to have devotions that dazzle you with the glory and grace of your great God! After all, that's the purpose of devotions—to be dazzled by an awesome view of the grandest spectacle the world has ever seen—the majesty of the Almighty God, the Creator of the Universe!

CHAPTER 1

God's Overwhelming Mercies

Today's Devotional Passage—Romans 11:33-12:2

Paul's Pleading with Believers

Sometimes we overlook small but significant things in Scripture. One example is found in Romans 11:33-12:2. Read it in your own Bible.

Paul pleads that we do three things in this passage:

- Give our bodies to God as living sacrifices
- Not be "shaped" like the world
- Be transformed by the renewed mind

These three phrases can be reduced to three words: surrender, separation, and transformation.

Surrender Our Bodies

First, we are urged to surrender or give our bodies to the Lord. This is something that every believer should do. God's great love for us demands complete surrender to Him, and failure to do so will actually keep us from enjoying God! His command to surrender is part of His love. He wants us to surrender to Him because His way is best for us.

Separate from the World

Second, Paul commands us to not be shaped like this world. Someone has paraphrased this command as "don't be pressed into the world's mold."

But what is "the world"? Briefly, "the world" or "worldliness" refers to living for the here-and-now. It is living as though this life (this world) is all there is to life. It is living as though there was no heaven and no existence beyond this life. This defines the lifestyle of the unsaved. They live for riches, wealth, fame, attention, and earthly power, with little regard for death. But believers are not to live like that. We are to live with eternity in view. We are to live as though this life is only the beginning, not the end!

Be Transformed by the Renewed Mind

Last, Paul encourages us to be transformed by the renewed mind. "Transformed" comes from the Greek word for "metamorphosis." We use this word to describe the changing of a caterpillar into a beautiful butterfly. "Transformation" then, speaks of a metamorphosis that takes place in a believer that changes (transforms) him or her from an ungodly person into a godly individual reflecting the very image of God!

Though that much is clear, a closer examination of the passage reveals an often-overlooked truth.

Surrender and separation to Him are natural reactions to being dazzled by His mercy and grace!

Because of God's Mercies

Paul pleads with us to do these three things because of the "mercies" (compassions) of the Lord. This is very important. We shouldn't do these three things simply because we are supposed to do them. We should do them because something compels us to do them. We should do them because we have an overwhelming desire to do them! But where does that overwhelming desire come from? The answer is seen in the little word *mercies*.

Paul's "therefore" in Romans 12 points backwards to God's mercies described in the first 11 chapters of Romans, and in particular to chapter 11. In other words, Paul bases his plea in Romans 12:1 on what the believer has learned about the mercies of God in chapters 1-11. Surrender, separation, and transformation find their motivation in the mercies of the Lord.

In the first 11 chapters we see that all men, at their very best, are sinners before a holy God (Rom. 3:23). Our sins have condemned us to die—for "the wages of sin is death" (Rom. 6:23). Yet, God provided a way out! He sent His precious Son to die for us on a cross that we might be saved (Rom. 5:6-8). Those who place their faith in Christ are "justified" (made innocent of their sin) and are "declared righteous" by God. Thus, believers have been graciously and mercifully saved from death and hell, and they have been given a home in heaven. Had God not done this, we would be hopelessly doomed to emptiness in this life and hell for all eternity.

Further, God gives believers, through the Holy Spirit, all they need to live a godly life (Rom. 6-8). He gives them power for service; He keeps them saved; and He will not let anything keep them from His love and eternal salvation (Rom. 8).

Paul concludes his review of God's mercies with these words of praise: "O the depth of the riches both of the wisdom and the knowledge of God! How unsearchable (untraceable) are His judgments and His ways past finding out! For of Him, and through Him, and to Him, are all things: to whom be the glory forever. Amen" (Rom. 11:33, 36). These words reveal Paul's own amazement with God's mercy.

Based on this awesome view of God and His mercies, Paul urges us to present our bodies to God, to turn from the distractions of this world, and to be transformed into His very image.

The problem is that we often think we should yield ourselves to the Lord and not be conformed to the world because "the Bible commands it." Actually, the Bible doesn't command us to "present/offer our bodies" to Him. Instead, Paul *begs* us to do so based on what we know of the mercies of God. In other words, we shouldn't surrender ourselves to the Lord because "we have to" but because we have an overwhelming desire to do so! Paul realizes that true surrender to the Lord doesn't come from mere obedience to commands. It comes from a heart that longs to surrender to the Lord because a person is overwhelmed by the awesomeness of God!

Until you are overwhelmed by His mercies and goodness, you will always struggle to yield yourself to the Lord and to separate from the world. You will constantly find the world more attractive than the Bible. Why? Because you have not been overwhelmed by Him.

Are you dazzled by God's mercy? Are you completely in awe of God's love in sending His Son to die for you on the cross, or are these merely facts you believe? Are you overcome with awe and deep devotion to God when you think of all He has done for you?

If not—you will not surrender to Him, nor will you determine to resist the powerful pull of the world.

Spend a few moments just thinking about the cross and all God has done for you.

Write some of God's mercies to you in the space provided.

CHAPTER 2

Hindrances to Transformation

Today's Devotional Passage—Romans 11:33-12:2

God made us to be dazzled, to be awestruck, to be amazed! That's why we love thrilling rides at an amusement park. That's why youth love skateboarding, fast cars, hard-driving music, adrenalin-pumping action movies, and extreme sports! Paul Tripp put it this way, "Teenagers need grand and glorious things in their lives. They want to be impressed. They love to be dazzled." Why, you might ask? Why did God make us to be dazzled? Because, God wanted us (as Tripp puts it) "to wonder and be overwhelmed by the glory and goodness and greatness of God. We're uniquely designed to respond to this awesome glory with worship, adoration, reverence, and being awestruck with God's glory. We're made for worship." (Paul David Tripp, "What is 'Success' in Parenting Teens?", JBC, Fall 2005, p. 18)

God wants you to be thrilled with Him. But sadly, that is not always the case. Christianity is not simply a religion to be practiced, or a creed to be believed! Christianity is about a Christ to be enjoyed, relished, and delighted in! We make too much of Christianity and not enough of Christ! Devotions should be thrilling because they are interacting with the Creator of the universe, the One who came to earth and died to save us from our sins!

Yielding to the Lord will be "reasonable" (Rom. 12:1) when seen in light of the splendor of our God and the overwhelming view of the cross! When we are awestruck by our God, then time with Him will dazzle us!

In the last chapter we learned that seeing the splendor and glory of His mercies turns boring devotions into dazzling devotions. In this chapter let's note a second truth in Romans 12:1-2.

Presenting our bodies to Him and separation from the world may not transform us into His image, but failure to do so can greatly hinder our transformation!

If you read this passage slowly, you will notice that we are transformed not by presenting our bodies, nor by separating from the world, but by *renewing our minds*! Transformation into the image of Christ does not come by merely dedicating ourselves to God, nor does it come by our efforts to not look like or act like the world! God's overwhelming mercies should motivate us to surrender and separate, but Paul informs us that it will only be by the renewing of our minds that we will become like Christ!

For example, a person can dedicate himself to be the next NBA superstar. But, making that decision does not automatically turn him into a 6-7" 270 pound leaper with ballet-like agility and athleticism! That can only come by a magical transformation!

Likewise, going forward in church, surrendering your body to the Lord, and making a commitment to separate from the world are good things, but they do not turn you into the next spiritual giant. Transformation comes only through a "renewed mind" and not through some decision you make at church.

However, that does not mean that surrendering our bodies to Him and separating from the world are unimportant. On the contrary, Paul urges us to do so. Why? Because failure to give ourselves to Him and failure to separate ourselves from the world will distract us from seeing God's transforming glory! It is hard to focus on two things at once. The more we focus on earthly things, the less we will focus on Him! Thus, we must be single-minded. That's why God says a "double-minded" person is unstable (James 1:8).

In other words, Romans 12:1-2 is really talking about our focus. Where is your mind most of the time? What do you think about the most? You will continually struggle in your Christian life as long as you keep your focus on earthly things. We must surrender our bodies to Him, not waste our bodies on self. And we should conform ourselves to Him, not spend all our waking moments thinking about self.

List some things that rob your mind of time to think about Him and to read His Word? Start with the obvious things like TV, cell phone texting, sports, etc. Be honest. List all the things that keep your mind off of God and His Word.

Most of these things are not wrong in themselves. But when they keep us from having a "renewed mind," they keep us from ever being transformed into the image of Christ! The battle in the Christian life is a battle for the mind. Either we use our bodies for self and fill our minds with thoughts on "this life" (the world), or we surrender our bodies and our minds to be filled with and focused on His mercies.

What fills your mind? What occupies most of your time? Spend a bit of time in prayer right now. Surrender yourself to Him. Determine to spend these next few months filling your mind with God's goodness and mercy!

CHAPTER 3

Renewing the Mind

Today's Devotional Passage—2 Corinthians 3:18

Read 2 Corinthians 3:18 slowly and note the following:

What are you to focus on when you read the Bible? _____

_____

_____

What will happen to you when you do this? _____

_____

_____

Thus far we have learned two things:

- In order to consistently live a surrendered and separated life, we must be overwhelmed by the mercies of God.

- The only way to be transformed into the image of Christ (to be like Christ) is through a renewed mind.

That naturally raises a single question. How can these things happen?

How can we be overwhelmed by His mercy? How do we develop a renewed mind? Interestingly, both questions have the same answer—by having a *right focus* when we read the Bible!

Focus is everything! The best athletes have the gift of focus! They are not easily distracted. So it is with devotions. What you focus on as you read the Bible is the key to a renewed mind and a transformed life.

Focus and a Renewed Mind

The word translated "renew" comes from two Greek words that mean "to be new again." It perhaps refers to being restored to the original mind that God gave Adam and Eve. Their minds were totally focused on God. They "communed" with Him morning and evening, and He was all they loved and cared for…until Satan entered the garden and changed their focus. He arrested their attention and dazzled them with the Tree of the Knowledge of Good and Evil. For the first time, Adam and Eve were distracted from God. Their focus changed to themselves and what God had forbidden them to eat. Suddenly, to have this knowledge of good and evil meant more to them than their relationship with God, and they ate the forbidden fruit sinning against God.

Through their sin, all men became sinners, and today we are born with a selfish, me-first mindset. But God made us to focus on His glory, not our own. Thus, He set up a plan to restore us to His original purpose. This plan took thousands of years, and eventually, in God's time, He sent Christ to save us through His death on the cross. Those who trust Him are given a new nature and enabled to once more see His glory!

But we don't live in a garden, and God doesn't visit us every day so that we can see Him. How, then, can we "see" God's glory today? That's where the Bible comes into focus! God gave us the Word to read so that we might daily see His glory. By doing so, our minds are renewed—made new again!

2 Corinthians 3:18 tells us how this happens. *1232*

If you answered the opening questions correctly, you saw that we are to look for one main thing in the Bible—the glory of God! You also learned that when you see His glory in the Word, the Holy Spirit will "transform" you into the same image you are beholding (God's glorious image). Thus, we learn the secret to a renewed mind, and thus, a transformed life!

It is to …

Focus on God's Glory in the Word

Sadly, some focus on everything but God's glory when they read the Bible!

- Some read it to learn facts about Biblical history.

- Some read it to learn about Bible characters (David, Elijah, Abraham, Moses, Paul, etc.).

- Some read it to see how they should behave or live.

- Some read it to find a verse to help them make a wise decision.

- Some read it to prove a point they are arguing.

While there is a time and place to do all of those things, they are not the primary reasons God wrote the Bible. Therefore, they should not be the primary reasons we read the Bible!

God primarily wrote the Bible to reveal His glory and grace. In John *1121* 5:39 Jesus tells us that the Bible is not about us, nor is it about how we should live. Rather, He tells us that the Bible is about Him! Thus, when we read the Bible, we should look for Him in it.

In your devotions these next few months, that's what you will learn how to do. And that's exciting because…

By Beholding Him in the Word, You Will Be Transformed

2 Corinthians 3:18 promises that as you "behold His glory" in the Bible you will be transformed! That is, your mind will be renewed, you will start thinking differently, you will start acting differently, and more and more you will become like Christ Himself! What an amazing promise. And all you do is look for Him—especially His glory and grace—in Scripture! The Holy Spirit will do the rest. He will gradually transform you into the image of Christ!

Are you ready for this to take place? Are you ready to start looking for God in Scripture? Are you ready to be dazzled by God's glory in your devotions?

Next we will begin in earnest. But remember....

This Is a Gradual Process

It won't happen instantly. 2 Corinthians 3:18 tells us that we are transformed "from glory to glory" or "with ever-increasing glory." So, don't expect to be transformed overnight! Don't even expect your devotions to be dazzling at first. This takes time. Over the next twelve weeks this booklet will lead you from very simple, God-focused devotions, to more complex devotions. If you are faithful, God will begin doing His amazing transforming work in you, little by little.

Stop now and once more surrender your body and mind to God. Prepare yourself to focus on God as you read His Word these next two months. Write your prayer on the lines below.

Weeks 1–2

Introduction

You are beginning a twelve-week adventure of discovery. You won't be discovering mere facts as you read your Bible. Instead, you will be discovering God. He gave us the Bible so that we can know and love Him. The first two weeks begin with very simple devotions. As you read the assigned passage, you will be looking for the answer to the question for that day. Don't be satisfied with just copying words onto a page. Think about the question and the Bible passage. What can you discover about the God who loves you and wants you to know Him? Each week you will have five passages assigned (Monday-Friday). Use the weekends to meditate on what you have learned or to catch up if you miss a day.

These devotions are a selection from *Manna 1*, a 12-month devotional published by Positive Action For Christ.

Instructions

For the next two weeks, your devotions will consist of two sections:

- The daily Probe section in which you will find a passage to be read and a question for each day that you are to answer
- A daily devotional form where you will record your daily devotional responses

Each day you will probe (read the question and the passage assigned). You will then ponder the passage (meditate) and record your answer to the probe. Finally, you will apply the truth learned by writing out how you plan to personalize it in your walk with the Lord that day. See the next page for an example.

Example

Monday, Date <u>September 9th</u>

Probe: <u>**What is my duty? Ecclesiastes 12:13-14**</u>

Ponder: <u>**How does the passage answer the question? I am to**</u>
fear God and to obey Him, for God knows everything I think
and do and will judge me for it.

Personalize: <u>**How can I apply this passage to my life? I must**</u>
learn to stand in awe of my God. I'm afraid I don't fear Him
enough. In fact, I need to fill my mind with Him so I will
think of His all-seeing eye when I am tempted to sin. I must
also realize He sees what I do and will reward me when I do
right.

Tuesday, Date

Probe:

Ponder:

Personalize:

Devotional Passages

Week One Probes:

- Monday—Do numbers limit God's work? 1 Samuel 14:1–15
- Tuesday—What should I seek? Zephaniah 2:1
- Wednesday—How did God save me? Titus 3:1–7
- Thursday—Who is always the same? Hebrews 13:7–9
- Friday—When I sin, whom do I sin against? Psalm 51:1–6

Week Two Probes:

- Monday—Who gives me ability and skill? Exodus 31:1–11
- Tuesday—How can I develop love in my heart for others? 1 John 4:7–11
- Wednesday—What should be my delight and counsel? Psalm 119:17–24
- Thursday—Who gives wisdom? Proverbs 2:6–9
- Friday—Whom should I exalt? 2 Corinthians 4:1–7

Monday, Date _____

Probe: _____

Ponder: _____

_____

_____

_____

_____

_____

_____

Personalize: _____

_____

_____

_____

_____

_____

_____

Tuesday, Date _____

Probe: _____

Ponder: _____

_____

_____

_____

_____

_____

Personalize: _____

_____

_____

_____

_____

_____

Wednesday, Date _____

Probe: _____

Ponder: _____

_____

_____

_____

_____

_____

Personalize: _____

_____

_____

_____

_____

_____

Thursday, Date _____

Probe: _____

Ponder: _____

_____

_____

_____

_____

Personalize: _____

_____

_____

_____

_____

_____

Friday, Date _____

Probe: _____

Ponder: _____

_____

_____

_____

_____

_____

Personalize: _____

_____

_____

_____

_____

_____

_____

Monday, Date _____

Probe: _____

Ponder: _____

_____

_____

_____

_____

_____

Personalize: _____

_____

_____

_____

_____

_____

Tuesday, Date

Probe: _____

Ponder: _____

_____

_____

_____

_____

_____

_____

Personalize: _____

_____

_____

_____

_____

_____

_____

Wednesday, Date

Probe: _____

Ponder: _____

_____

_____

_____

_____

_____

_____

Personalize: _____

_____

_____

_____

_____

_____

_____

Thursday, Date _____

Probe: _____

Ponder: _____

_____
_____
_____
_____
_____
_____

Personalize: _____

_____
_____
_____
_____
_____
_____

Friday, Date _____

Probe: _____

Ponder: _____

_____
_____
_____
_____
_____
_____

Personalize: _____

_____
_____
_____
_____
_____
_____

Weeks 3–4

Introduction

Your devotions for the next two weeks are similar to the previous weeks. However, instead of a single Probe, you will have two questions daily. The second question helps you focus on how what you have learned about God can affect your life. While change is not the main goal of reading the Bible, as you see God for who He is, you will find that you are being changed into His image just as we studied in chapter three.

You will find that the devotions will get progressively more complex and God-focused as we proceed over the coming weeks. Yet no matter how simple or difficult your method of Bible study, the primary purpose is to see God. Whether you are reading a passage for the first time or working through it for the hundredth time, God wants to reveal Himself to you. Look for Him!

These devotions are taken from *Manna 2*, a 12-month devotional published by Positive Action For Christ.

Instructions

The forms this week look very similar to the forms from weeks one and two. Because there are now two probes, you will not need to write them out on the weekly sheet. Instead, record the passage that you are reading. Be sure to keep the probe questions in mind as you are reading.

Fill in the blanks as follows:

- Date: Insert the day that you completed the devotional reading and form.
- Passage: Insert the text you are reading for that day.

- Ponder: What does the assigned passage teach me about God? How does it show His character or attributes?
- Personalize: How do the truths you just learned about God influence your life? How can you praise God for these works or attributes? How will this new knowledge of God influence your relationship with Him and with others?

Example

Monday, Date <u>September 23rd</u>

Passage: <u>John 4:1-38</u>

Ponder: <u>Christ was most satisfied when He was doing the work</u> <u>of the Father. In this passage, He was doing that work as</u> <u>He showed the Samaritan woman how she could know and</u> <u>worship the true God. God is not worshiped by religious</u> <u>traditions. He is worshiped in spirit and in truth. He wants</u> <u>our heart worship at all times and in all places.</u>

Personalize: <u>I will find the true purpose of my life as I grow in</u> <u>my knowledge and worship of God. Part of that worship is</u> <u>testifying to others of the glory of God and His wonderful</u> <u>gift of salvation through His Son.</u>

Tuesday, Date

Passage:

Ponder:

Personalize:

Devotional Passages

Monday—Daniel 1:1–21

- These young Jewish men were in Babylon because of Judah's idolatry. What does God's activity in their lives show about His character?
- In what areas of my life am I making hard decisions because I want to be faithful to my God?

Tuesday—Daniel 2:1–23

- How does Daniel demonstrate spiritual leadership?
- In what areas of my life have I failed to praise God for His provision?

Wednesday—Daniel 2:25–49

- What might have been God's purpose in revealing the dream to Daniel?
- How can I demonstrate the kind of confidence in God that Daniel had?

Thursday—Daniel 3:1–30

- What does the young men's answer to Nebuchadnezzar in verses 16–19 indicate about their focus?
- How is my view of God similar to or different from Nebuchadnezzar's?

Friday—Daniel 4:1–37

- How would I describe the change in Nebuchadnezzar's view of God?
- How do I actively give God credit for my accomplishments?

Week Four Probes:

Monday—Psalm 89:1–18

- Describe the central feature of God's character in this passage.

- What implications does this divine quality have for my life and the way I live it?

Tuesday—Psalm 95:1–11

- What does worship have to do with bowing down and kneeling before the Lord?

- In what ways do I need to soften my heart and stop testing the Lord?

Wednesday—Psalm 96:1–13

- What three words might best summarize the attitude this passage says I should have towards the Lord?

- What kinds of events or circumstances cause me to lose this attitude?

Thursday—Psalm 97:1–12

- How do God's righteousness and judgment provide a sound foundation for His throne?

- Do I acknowledge my shame when I set up material idols over God, or am I going to face shame in the future? Why?

Friday—Psalm 98:1–9

- What do I learn about God in this passage?

- How has God shown His faithful love to me personally?

Monday, Date _____

Passage: _____

Ponder: _____

_____

_____

_____

_____

_____

Personalize: _____

_____

_____

_____

_____

_____

_____

Tuesday, Date _____

Passage: _____

Ponder: _____

_____

_____

_____

_____

_____

Personalize: _____

_____

_____

_____

_____

_____

Wednesday, Date

Passage: _____

Ponder: _____

_____

_____

_____

_____

_____

_____

Personalize: _____

_____

_____

_____

_____

_____

_____

Thursday, Date

Passage: _____

Ponder: _____

_____

_____

_____

_____

_____

Personalize: _____

_____

_____

_____

_____

_____

Friday, Date _____

Passage: _____

Ponder: _____
_____
_____
_____
_____
_____
_____

Personalize: _____
_____
_____
_____
_____
_____
_____

Monday, Date _____

Passage: _____

Ponder: _____
_____
_____
_____
_____
_____
_____

Personalize: _____
_____
_____
_____
_____
_____
_____

Tuesday, Date

Passage: _____

Ponder: _____

_____

_____

_____

_____

_____

_____

Personalize: _____

_____

_____

_____

_____

_____

_____

Wednesday, Date

Passage: _____

Ponder: _____

_____

_____

_____

_____

_____

Personalize: _____

_____

_____

_____

_____

_____

Thursday, Date _____

Passage: _____

Ponder: _____
_____
_____
_____
_____
_____
_____

Personalize: _____
_____
_____
_____
_____
_____
_____

Friday, Date _____

Passage: _____

Ponder: _____
_____
_____
_____
_____
_____
_____

Personalize: _____
_____
_____
_____
_____
_____
_____

Weeks 5-6

Introduction

The first four weeks of *God-Focused Devotions* used short passages of Scripture to introduce you to simple concepts of looking for God in Scripture. The next two weeks will be a bit more challenging. Now you will carefully examine a short book in the Bible to squeeze as much out of it as you can about your great God.

Are you ready to take the next step? Follow the instructions, take your time, and be patient. Even though this method may seem frustrating at first, if you apply yourself diligently and consistently, you will continue to know your God more intimately. Obviously, the task cannot be accomplished in two quick weeks, but if you continue these disciplines over time, you will grow to know Him and then to love, adore, and worship Him.

These devotions are adapted from *Manna 3*, a 12-month devotional published by Positive Action For Christ.

Instructions

The next two weeks guide you through some basic Bible study techniques. During week five, you will be looking for major themes in the book of Philippians. As you read, watch for words or phrases that are repeated within each chapter and the book as a whole. Also look for different words that have the same meaning (i.e., power, might, and strength). To remind you to continue to focus on God as you are reading, additional space is provided to you to note truth you may discover about God's work and character.

Week six focuses on the work of God. Begin each day by recording how you see God at work in the chapter. Then note the ways God is working in your life according to what you have read. The third question helps you personalize the truths you discover as you consider how you need to respond to God's works. Finally, take time to list things from the passage and from your life for which you want to thank the Lord.

Devotional Passages

Monday

Read Philippians chapter 1 two times, looking for words or phrases that are repeated. Also, look for words that have similar meanings.

What do these repeated words suggest about what are the most important issues in this chapter?

What can you learn about God's character or His works in this chapter?

Tuesday

Read Philippians chapter 2 two times, looking for words or phrases that are repeated. Also, look for words that have similar meaning.

What do these repeated words suggest about what are the most important issues in this chapter?

What can you learn about God's character or His works in this chapter?

Wednesday

Read Philippians chapter 3 two times, looking for words or phrases that are repeated. Also, look for words that have similar meaning.

What do these repeated words suggest about what are the most important issues in this chapter?

What can you learn about God's character or His works in this chapter?

Thursday

Read Philippians chapter 4 two times, looking for words or phrases that are repeated. Also, look for words that have similar meaning.

What do these repeated words suggest about what are the most important issues in this chapter?

What can you learn about God's character or His works in this chapter?

Read back through the book of Philippians. Record below some major themes you have discovered from your word study.

Monday

Read Philippians chapter 1 again. List below every way that you can see God at work in the chapter.

How do these things that God does have an impact on your life?

How should your attitude toward God be affected as you consider the work He is doing in your life?

What do you need to thank Him for today?

Read Philippians chapter 2 again. List every way that you can see God at work in the chapter.

How do these things that God does have an impact on your life?

How should your attitude toward God be affected as you consider the work He is doing in your life?

What do you need to thank Him for today?

Wednesday

Read Philippians chapter 3 again. List below every way that you can see God at work in the chapter.

How do these things that God does have an impact on your life?

How should your attitude toward God be affected as you consider the work He is doing in your life?

What do you need to thank Him for today?

Thursday

Read Philippians chapter 4 again. List below every way that you can see God at work in the chapter.

How do these things that God does have an impact on your life?

How should your attitude toward God be affected as you consider the work He is doing in your life?

What do you need to thank Him for today?

Friday

Read back through the book of Philippians. Record below some major truths you have learned from this week's study of how God works.

Weeks 7–8

Introduction

After finishing the last two weeks of devotions, you may have noticed that there is much more to a Bible passage than first meets the eye. Most of us read on a factual level. That is, we merely gather facts from whatever we are reading. This is important, but when reading the Bible, there is much more for us to see. In addition to the factual information, there are theological and doctrinal truths to be grasped and digested. As we learned in the introductory chapters, the theological truths (truths about the Person and work of God) are actually at the heart of what is written. Of course, all these truths will have a profound effect on you individually as you meditate on God and apply the truths of His Word.

These devotions are taken from *Manna 4*, a 12-month devotional published by Positive Action For Christ.

Instructions

The next two weeks will help you further refine the way you read your Bible. Each day you will read a short passage four times, each time looking for something different.

- Factual: The first reading we call Factual. You should read the passage fast in order to get a quick overview of exactly what happens in the passage (what it is about) and then record the basic idea of the passage (i.e., Jesus healed a man on the Sabbath and was criticized for it).

- Theological: The second reading we call Theological. Read the passage again, this time more slowly, and look for every truth you can find about God the Father, God the Son, and God the Holy Spirit. Record everything you see about His character and attributes, how He works and thinks, His pu. poses and plans, what He does, etc.

- Doctrinal: The third reading we call Doctrinal. Read the passage again to discover other truths that are there—perhaps something about salvation, spiritual growth, sin, Satan, the Church, prayer, the gospel, witnessing, etc.

- Practical: After the fourth reading, consider how the theology and doctrine in the passage should impact your life today. List some specific ways you can apply the principles you have learned to your life.

After each reading, record your thoughts and insights in the appropriate section. The following page provides an example of what to look for in God's Word and how to use the forms. Be God-focused in your approach to His revelation of Himself. Don't study the Word of God; study the God of the Word!

Example

Passage: **Ephesians 2:1-10**   Date: **March 17**

FACTUAL (what the Bible states/what happens in this passage):

All of us are born spiritually dead in our sins with no hope for salvation apart from God's grace.

THEOLOGICAL (what I learn about the Father, the Son, or the Holy Spirit):

Verse 4: God is rich in mercy and grace.
Verse 4: God loves us even before we love Him.
Verse 5: God is the giver of spiritual life.
Verse 7: God saves us to bring attention to Himself.
Verse 8: God offers salvation as a gift.
Verse 10: God created us.

DOCTRINAL (truths I see about salvation, spiritual growth, sin, Satan, the Church, prayer, the gospel, witnessing, etc.):

Verse 2: I was born a sinner, it is part of my nature, and it causes me to be spiritually dead.
Verse 3: Satan is now working in the world all around us.
Verse 3: All people are born sinners and are, by nature, "children of wrath."
Verse 5: Salvation is a work of God through which He literally makes me alive.
Verse 6: When we are saved we are placed "in Christ Jesus."

PRACTICAL (lessons I should apply to how I live today):

Verses 2-3: I need to make sure, through God's power, that my life no longer resembles the characteristics of the unsaved person.
Verses 5-6: I need to meditate often on the power, love, and grace of God, which I have experienced firsthand as a child of God.
Verse 9: I did nothing to earn my salvation so my spirit and attitude should be one of humility.
Because God has chosen to save me, I need to share this wonderful message of salvation with others.

Devotional Passages

Week Seven Passages:

Monday—Mark 1:35-45

Tuesday—Mark 2:1–12

Wednesday—Mark 2:13–22

Thursday—Mark 2:23–28

Friday—Mark 3:1–12

Week Eight Passages:

Monday—Romans 8:29–39

Tuesday—Romans 9:1–13

Wednesday—Romans 9:15–33

Thursday—Romans 10:1–13

Friday—Romans 10:15–21

assage:	Date:

FACTUAL (what the Bible states/what happens in this passage):

THEOLOGICAL (what I learn about the Father, the Son, or the Holy Spirit):

DOCTRINAL (truths I see about salvation, spiritual growth, sin, Satan, the Church, prayer, the gospel, witnessing, etc.):

PRACTICAL (lessons I should apply to how I live today):

Passage:	Date:

FACTUAL (what the Bible states/what happens in this passage):

THEOLOGICAL (what I learn about the Father, the Son, or the Holy Spirit):

DOCTRINAL (truths I see about salvation, spiritual growth, sin, Satan, the Church, prayer, the gospel, witnessing, etc.):

PRACTICAL (lessons I should apply to how I live today):

Passage:	Date:

FACTUAL (what the Bible states/what happens in this passage):

THEOLOGICAL (what I learn about the Father, the Son, or the Holy Spirit):

DOCTRINAL (truths I see about salvation, spiritual growth, sin, Satan, the Church, prayer, the gospel, witnessing, etc.):

PRACTICAL (lessons I should apply to how I live today):

Passage:	Date:

FACTUAL (what the Bible states/what happens in this passage):

THEOLOGICAL (what I learn about the Father, the Son, or the Holy Spirit):

DOCTRINAL (truths I see about salvation, spiritual growth, sin, Satan, the Church, prayer, the gospel, witnessing, etc.):

PRACTICAL (lessons I should apply to how I live today):

assage:	Date:

FACTUAL (what the Bible states/what happens in this passage):

THEOLOGICAL (what I learn about the Father, the Son, or the Holy Spirit):

DOCTRINAL (truths I see about salvation, spiritual growth, sin, Satan, the Church, prayer, the gospel, witnessing, etc.):

PRACTICAL (lessons I should apply to how I live today):

Passage:	Date:

FACTUAL (what the Bible states/what happens in this passage):

THEOLOGICAL (what I learn about the Father, the Son, or the Holy Spirit):

DOCTRINAL (truths I see about salvation, spiritual growth, sin, Satan, the Church, prayer, the gospel, witnessing, etc.):

PRACTICAL (lessons I should apply to how I live today):

Passage:	Date:

FACTUAL (what the Bible states/what happens in this passage):

THEOLOGICAL (what I learn about the Father, the Son, or the Holy Spirit):

DOCTRINAL (truths I see about salvation, spiritual growth, sin, Satan, the Church, prayer, the gospel, witnessing, etc.):

PRACTICAL (lessons I should apply to how I live today):

Passage:	Date:

FACTUAL (what the Bible states/what happens in this passage):

THEOLOGICAL (what I learn about the Father, the Son, or the Holy Spirit):

DOCTRINAL (truths I see about salvation, spiritual growth, sin, Satan, the Church, prayer, the gospel, witnessing, etc.):

PRACTICAL (lessons I should apply to how I live today):

Passage:	Date:

FACTUAL (what the Bible states/what happens in this passage):

THEOLOGICAL (what I learn about the Father, the Son, or the Holy Spirit):

DOCTRINAL (truths I see about salvation, spiritual growth, sin, Satan, the Church, prayer, the gospel, witnessing, etc.):

PRACTICAL (lessons I should apply to how I live today):

Passage:	Date:

FACTUAL (what the Bible states/what happens in this passage):

THEOLOGICAL (what I learn about the Father, the Son, or the Holy Spirit):

DOCTRINAL (truths I see about salvation, spiritual growth, sin, Satan, the Church, prayer, the gospel, witnessing, etc.):

PRACTICAL (lessons I should apply to how I live today):

Passage:	Date:

FACTUAL (what the Bible states/what happens in this passage):

THEOLOGICAL (what I learn about the Father, the Son, or the Holy Spirit):

DOCTRINAL (truths I see about salvation, spiritual growth, sin, Satan, the Church, prayer, the gospel, witnessing, etc.):

PRACTICAL (lessons I should apply to how I live today):

Passage:	Date:

FACTUAL (what the Bible states/what happens in this passage):

THEOLOGICAL (what I learn about the Father, the Son, or the Holy Spirit):

DOCTRINAL (truths I see about salvation, spiritual growth, sin, Satan, the Church, prayer, the gospel, witnessing, etc.):

PRACTICAL (lessons I should apply to how I live today):

Passage:	Date:

FACTUAL (what the Bible states/what happens in this passage):

THEOLOGICAL (what I learn about the Father, the Son, or the Holy Spirit):

DOCTRINAL (truths I see about salvation, spiritual growth, sin, Satan, the Church, prayer, the gospel, witnessing, etc.):

PRACTICAL (lessons I should apply to how I live today):

Passage:	Date:

FACTUAL (what the Bible states/what happens in this passage):

THEOLOGICAL (what I learn about the Father, the Son, or the Holy Spirit):

DOCTRINAL (truths I see about salvation, spiritual growth, sin, Satan, the Church, prayer, the gospel, witnessing, etc.):

PRACTICAL (lessons I should apply to how I live today):

Weeks 9–10

Introduction

The Pharisees studied the Old Testament with a fervor few have ever had. They dissected every letter and word, but they failed to see what it was all about. Jesus rebuked them by saying that though they studied the Word diligently, they didn't see Him in it (John 5:39). Sadly, they saw everything in the Old Testament except what they were supposed to see. Can that be said of us?

The songwriter captured the essence of true devotions with these words,

> *Turn your eyes upon Jesus!*
> *Look full in His wonderful face,*
> *and the things of earth will grow strangely dim,*
> *in the light of His glory and grace.*

For the next two weeks you will have an opportunity to do just that. Taking what you have learned in the last few weeks of Bible study, you will turn your eyes fully upon God—His attributes, His character, and His works. Remember, when we speak of God we're speaking of the entire Godhead: God the Father, God the Son (the Lord Jesus Christ), and God the Holy Spirit.

The following devotions are taken from *Manna 5*, a 12–month devotional produced by Positive Action For Christ.

Instructions

As you read the assigned passage each day, you will be looking for three different aspects of God's Person and work: What God does, Who God is, and How God works. Record your observations in the spaces provided. A word of explanation on these three categories is in order:

What God Does: In this section, list the obvious actions God takes in the passage. Even simple things need to be recorded: "He spoke, He walked, He sat, He saw, etc." When you fail to see any evident work that God/Christ accomplished, read the passage again and look for God's providential hand. His plan is at work even in those passages that do not mention Him directly.

Who God Is: In this section of the form, record what you learn about God's character and person (His attributes—He is sovereign, He is omniscient, He is compassionate, He is interested in us, He is involved in our lives, etc.) Again, you may have to think about the big picture to see His character, but it *is* there! Carefully reading and pondering a passage to find all that you can about the Lord is called "meditation." Work at it, and you will be blessed (Psalm 1:1–2).

How God Works: This may be the most difficult element to see. It will require you to step back and look at the entire passage as one whole unit. What does the passage show about how God does things (He takes His time, He works when we don't know He is working, He prepares things ahead of time, He never sleeps, etc.)?

Example

Passage: **1 Kings 17:8–16**	Date: **March 3**

Focus On God

What does God do in this passage?

Spoke to Elijah—vs. 8
Gave directions to Elijah—vs. 9
Prepared a total stranger for him—vs. 9
Caused their paths to meet—vs. 10
Promised the widow her food would last—vs. 14
Kept His promise—vs. 16
Miraculously supplied all the widow needed to support God's prophet

What does God reveal about Himself in this passage?

Personal, involved, immanent
Sovereign, Lord
Provider/sovereign in our lives
God of providence
Divine arranger
Faithful, true
Omnipotent sustainer

What does this passage teach about how God works?

1. Often waits until the very last moment to work and in that way tests our faith—vss. 7–9. (He waited until the water completely dried in the brook.)
2. He prepares the road ahead of us.—vs. 9
3. He often uses unconventional means to care for us (a woman, widow, stranger, foreigner, heathen; a poor, unknown person).
4. He will never let us lack when we are obedient to His will.
5. He acts for our good and for His glory.

Devotional Passages

Week Nine Passages:

Monday—John 16:1–11

Tuesday—John 16:12–22

Wednesday—John 16:23–33

Thursday—John 17:1–12

Friday—John 17:13–26

Week Ten Passages:

Monday—Isaiah 6:1–13

Tuesday—Isaiah 7:1–9

Wednesday—Isaiah 7:10–25

Thursday—Isaiah 8:1–10

Friday—Isaiah 8:11–22

Passage:	Date:

Focus On God

What does God do in this passage?

What does God reveal about Himself in this passage?

What does this passage teach about how God works?

Passage:	Date:

Focus On God

What does God do in this passage?

What does God reveal about Himself in this passage?

What does this passage teach about how God works?

Passage:	Date:

Focus On God

What does God do in this passage?

What does God reveal about Himself in this passage?

What does this passage teach about how God works?

Passage:	Date:

Focus On God

What does God do in this passage?

What does God reveal about Himself in this passage?

What does this passage teach about how God works?

Passage:	Date:

Focus On God

What does God do in this passage?

What does God reveal about Himself in this passage?

What does this passage teach about how God works?

Passage:	Date:

Focus On God

What does God do in this passage?

What does God reveal about Himself in this passage?

What does this passage teach about how God works?

Passage:	Date:

Focus On God

What does God do in this passage?

What does God reveal about Himself in this passage?

What does this passage teach about how God works?

Passage:	Date:

Focus On God

What does God do in this passage?

What does God reveal about Himself in this passage?

What does this passage teach about how God works?

Passage:	Date:

Focus On God

What does God do in this passage?

What does God reveal about Himself in this passage?

What does this passage teach about how God works?

Passage:	Date:

Focus On God

What does God do in this passage?

What does God reveal about Himself in this passage?

What does this passage teach about how God works?

Weeks 11–12

Introduction

As you draw to the end of your twelve-week adventure, you have learned much about both the Word of God and the God of the Word. Whether you have been reading your Bible for years or you have just made a decision to give serious attention to daily study of the Word of God, this book has been developed to help you spend time with your Lord. For the past 10 weeks you have been progressively learning how to focus on God in your daily devotions. You are now reaching "graduate level!"

The next two weeks we turn our attention to a key element in understanding God's Word. The Bible is not a collection of books. It is one book, written by one Author with one story. Second Timothy 3:16 tells us that the Bible was "God-breathed" (written by God), and God has written His Book with a single overriding story. That story we call *The Story of His Glory*. Everything God does is for His glory (Romans 11:36). He made the earth for His glory. He made mankind for His glory. And He wrote the Bible to reveal His glory. The Bible is not about us but about Him! As we read it, therefore, we should look for Him rather than for us! We should ask, "What does this passage teach about God's glory and about His grace?"

The following devotions are part of *Manna 6*, a 12–month devotional produced by Positive Action For Christ.

Instructions

The forms you will use for the next two weeks are designed to help you focus on *The Story of His Glory*. Each week you will begin with a background reading designed to help you see the aspects of *The*

Story of His Glory. You will then read the assigned passage once daily recording your thoughts in the following areas:

- What God Does: First, record in a few words what God does in the passage you just read. Look carefully as you read so that you can list all the things you see God do in the passage, even when His name is not specifically mentioned. Summarize what God does in a sentence or two.

- His Glory: Under "His Glory," record the various ways you see God's attributes, works, and ways displayed in the passage. For example, you might see God's sovereignty in calling Moses to free His people from Egypt, His omnipotence in parting the Red Sea, etc.

- His Grace: Under "His Grace," record how you see the following:
  - God's gracious works (doing for man what he doesn't deserve)
  - God's grace in salvation, the cross, God's plan of redemption, and Christ. Naturally, if you are reading this from the Old Testament, you will have to see "pictures" of His salvation, of Christ, of the cross, and of the Gospel. For example, you might see God's saving grace in the ark, or in the Old Testament offerings and sacrifices, or in Abraham offering up his son Isaac.

- Other Thoughts: Under "Other Thoughts," note any thoughts that don't seem to fit into the other categories.

The following background stories and devotional forms are taken from *Manna 6*, a 12–month devotional produced by Positive Action For Christ. A sample is provided on the next page.

Example

The Story of His Glory • The Plan of Redemption	
Passage: **Exodus 9:1-7**	Date: **July 11** ☒ Background read

What God does in this passage

Spoke to Moses - vs. 1
Told him where to go and what to say - vs. 1
Warned Pharaoh of the consequences of disobedience - vss. 2-3
Set a definite time for Pharaoh to act - vs. 5
Kept His word (promise) - vs. 6
Killed Egypt's livestock, but kept Israel's cattle alive - vs 6

His Glory: What you learned about the character and attributes of God in this passage

Sovereign - controls what lives and what dies
Faithful - kept His promise
Involved in our lives
Source of Life - God is "Life" as He gives life and takes life as He
desires
Omnipotent - had the power to destroy the livestock of one nation
while preserving the livestock of another nation
Omniscient - knew what would happen and when it would happen

His Grace: What you learned about God's grace, Christ, the cross, and the Gospel in this passage

God was gracious to warn Pharaoh, despite Pharaoh's sinfulness
(likewise, God faithfully warns unbelievers today of their need of
Christ)
God gave Pharaoh time to respond - God has given sinners 2,000
years to repent because He is not willing that any should perish

Other Thoughts

Pharaoh's unbelief is amazing. In spite of all he has seen God do,
He still hardens his heart - Am I like this? Do I listen to God's
warnings?

Devotional Passages

Week Eleven Passages:

Monday—Read the Background Story for Genesis 1–2.

Tuesday–Friday—Read Genesis 1–2 daily and fill in the form as you read. Each day you will see things you missed the day before and can add to your growing notes. We have included an extra form in case you completely fill in a section and need more room to write your thoughts and insights.

Background Story—Genesis 1-2

Genesis is called the "book of beginnings" (the "Genesis" of all things). In this book you will find the beginning of most things we know. In this book we see the beginning of the universe; of our world and all that is in it; of the human race, the family, and the animal kingdom; of the promise and line of Christ; of the Jewish race; and of God's covenants with Noah, Abraham, and Moses.

Perhaps the sovereignty and power of God are nowhere more clearly seen than in this book. Here we discover that God is the one true God who made us, who owns us, who set up the laws that govern nature, who controls all of history, and who has designed all things for His glory.

The Story of His Glory begins in Genesis 1-2, which you will read through four times this week. Perhaps no passage of Scripture has been more attacked and ridiculed than these two chapters. Man doesn't want a God who created all things. Why? If there is such a God, then man is subject to Him. Man wants to be his own god. He doesn't want to answer to another. Thus, in man's determination to run his own life, he denies the existence of a creator God who controls the universe and who owns the life of each man in it. Yet, to assume that all we see happened by chance is ultimately more irrational than to simply believe there is a God who created it with design and purpose. Romans 1 states that God created our world to reveal His glory. As you read through Genesis 1-2 this week look for

...ne glorious things you learn about your God, and then look for the gracious things you see in Him.

The Story of His Glory • The Plan of Redemption

Passage:

Date:

☐ Background read

What God does in this passage

His Glory: What you learned about the character and attributes of God in this passage

HIs Grace: What you learned about God's grace, Christ, the cross, and the Gospel in this passage

Other Thoughts

The Story of His Glory • The Plan of Redemption

Passage:

Date:

☐ Background read

What God does in this passage

His Glory: What you learned about the character and attributes of God in this passage

HIs Grace: What you learned about God's grace, Christ, the cross, and the Gospel in this passage

Other Thoughts

Monday—Read the Background Story for Genesis 3-4.

Tuesday-Friday—Read Genesis 3–4 daily and fill in the form as you read. Each day you will see things you missed the day before and can add to your growing notes. We have included an extra form in case you completely fill in a section and need more room to write your thoughts and insights.

Background Story—Genesis 3-4

Genesis 3 addresses a specific question: How will the man and woman God created respond to His grace, love, and provision of all they need? God gave them a test by placing a single prohibition before them. He allowed them to eat of any tree in the garden but one—the tree of the knowledge of good and evil. How would they respond?

After some time (we are not told how long), Satan appeared in the form of a talking serpent. Satan's purpose was single—to rob God of His glory. Remember, history is *The Story of His Glory*. But Satan would have it be the story of his (Satan's) glory. Isaiah 14:12-15 indicates that sometime after his creation Satan's heart was filled with pride, and he coveted God's glory for himself. Some Bible scholars suggest that the creation of mankind may have been the very thing that led him to the jealousy and pride that caused his fall (1 Timothy 3:6).

Since Satan could not create a physical form by his own power, he had to take possession of a creature God had made. The serpent fit his purposes. The serpent began with a question, a method Satan still uses today. His tactics were simple—to get Eve's focus off of the good things God had provided (to take her attention away from God's glory and grace) and to get her to think about the one thing she couldn't do. The same is true today. Satan does not want us enjoying God's glory and grace. His desire is that we be dissatisfied with what we don't have. Ultimately, Eve's distraction from God brought about her fall and the fall of Adam and all mankind. As you read this story ach day this week, keep your focus on the wonderful things you see about God's glory and God's grace.

Sin destroyed God's ultimate purpose in creation—to create a people to praise and glorify Him. Adam and Eve lost their relationship with the Lord. Their fallen nature now despised God, was wicked and depraved, and sought to satisfy self rather than to glorify God.

But even in their sin, God hinted at His grace. God created man to glorify Him, and though man had now fallen in sin and lost his capacity to glorify God, God had a plan. He would restore man to Himself and make him once more capable of bringing glory to the Creator. In Genesis 3:15 He promised that one day the "Seed of the woman" would crush Satan's (the serpent's) head. Who was this promised Seed of the woman? As we shall see, it was Jesus Christ, who would be born of a woman (Mary) thousands of years later. But aren't all men born of a woman? Yes, but all men are the seed of their father, not their mother. Though moms give birth, the child is the seed of the father. The phrase, seed of a woman, is thus a very special statement. It hints at a Virgin Birth.

So, the subplot begins. *The Story of His Glory* will now focus on God's eternal plan for mankind's restoration. We call it The Plan of Redemption. God will institute this plan to restore (redeem or purchase back) man to the position for which Adam and Eve were originally created. God will not be thwarted by Satan. He will one day send a Redeemer to earth to pay for mankind's sin and to eventually restore them to Adam's previous innocence. The rest of the Bible reveals that story.

Chapter 4 reveals the results of Adam and Eve's sin on their children when Cain murders his brother Abel out of jealousy. God desires to bless us, but sin and Satan rob us of that blessing. Cain shows what the fallen man looks like—the seed of the father. Due to Adam's sin all men became sinful (Romans 5:12), as seen in Adam's murderous son Cain. As you read this chapter, think of how gracious God was to Cain—even in his sin.

Part of God's Plan of Redemption was for the Seed of the woman (Christ) to eventually come to earth and die on a cross for mankind, but that part of the story is yet unknown to Adam and Eve and their children. God will gradually reveal the plan over the coming centuries.

First, He teaches Cain and Abel that they were to make offerings to God. The offerings had to include the shedding of blood. For "without the shedding of blood there is no remission (putting away of sin)" (Hebrews 9:22). When God rejected Cain's offering (which did not include shed blood), Cain became very angry. Note how he responded—by shedding the blood of his brother, Abel. Thus, *The Story of His Glory* has something to do with shed blood. The Plan of Redemption has begun—and the coming centuries will tell the rest of the story.

Passage:

Date:

☐ Background read

What God does in this passage

His Glory: What you learned about the character and attributes of God in this passage

HIs Grace: What you learned about God's grace, Christ, the cross, and the Gospel in this passage

Other Thoughts

The Story of His Glory • The Plan of Redemption

Passage:

Date:

☐ Background read

What God does in this passage

His Glory: What you learned about the character and attributes of God in this passage

HIs Grace: What you learned about God's grace, Christ, the cross, and the Gospel in this passage

Other Thoughts

Optional Group Study Guide

Pastors, teachers, and parents may find it helpful to work through this book with their students or children. To help facilitate a group study, we suggest weekly meetings on the following schedule:

Meeting 1	Discuss Preface; Assign Chapter 1
Meeting 2	Discuss Chapter 1; Assign Chapter 2
Meeting 3	Discuss Chapter 2; Assign Chapter 3
Meeting 4	Discuss Chapter 3 and Introduction to Weeks 1–2; Assign Week 1 Devotions
Meeting 5	Discuss Week 1 Devotions; Assign Week 2 Devotions
Meeting 6	Discuss Week 2 Devotions and Introduction to Weeks 3–4; Assign Week 3 Devotions
Meeting 7	Discuss Week 3 Devotions; Assign Week 4 Devotions
Meeting 8	Discuss Week 4 Devotions and Introduction to Weeks 5–6; Assign Week 5 Devotions
Meeting 9	Discuss Week 5 Devotions; Assign Week 6 Devotions
Meeting 10	Discuss Week 6 Devotions and Introduction to Weeks 7–8; Assign Week 7 Devotions
Meeting 11	Discuss Week 7 Devotions; Assign Week 8 Devotions
Meeting 12	Discuss Week 8 Devotions and Introduction to Weeks 9–10; Assign Week 9 Devotions
Meeting 13	Discuss Week 9 Devotions; Assign Week 10 Devotions
Meeting 14	Discuss Week 10 Devotions and Introduction to Weeks 11–12; Assign Week 11 Devotions
Meeting 15	Discuss Week 11 Devotions; Assign Week 12 Devotions
Meeting 16	Discuss Week 12 Devotions